TEN YEARS IN
AN OPEN NECKED SHIRT

Freelance artist Steve Maguire was born in Barrow-in-Furness; in his mid-teens he left home to study at Manchester Art College.

His hedonistic existence took him to Mr Smith's, one of the many thriving juke joints on the northern club circuit that featured regular performances from the poet, John Cooper Clarke.

The two became inseparable friends while pursuing their respective careers and later pooled their considerable talents in the production of this book.

Steve's paintings were recently on exhibition at Salford City Art Gallery where they received critical acclaim and rapturous public response.

He now lives with his wife, Helen, and daughter, Lola, in a lay-by on the A5.

John Cooper Clarke

TEN YEARS IN AN OPEN NECKED SHIRT

Illustrated by Steve Maguire

to young macdonald
(the one without the farm)

An Arena Book

Published by Arrow Books Limited

62-65 Chandos Place, London WC2N 4NW

An imprint of Century Hutchinson Ltd

London Melbourne Sydney Auckland
Johannesburg and agencies throughout
the world

First published 1983
Reprinted 1984, 1985, 1986 and 1987

© April Music 1977, 1978, 1979,
1980, 1981, 1982, 1983

Illustrations © April Music 1982, 1983

Set in Linotron Univers Light by
Rowland Phototypesetting Ltd
Bury St Edmunds, Suffolk

Printed and bound in Great Britain by
Anchor Brendon Limited, Tiptree, Essex

ISBN 0 09 931240 9

Contents

ten years in an open necked shirt   7

euro communist/gucci socialist   10
the ghost of al capone   11
i mustn't go down to the sea again   14
the face behind the scream   15
90 degrees in my shades   18
psycle sluts: part one   20
psycle sluts: part two   22
the day my pad went M^{A}D   24
i married a monster from outer space   26
belladonna   28
i wanna be yours   30
readers' wives   32
i was a teenage werewolf – or was i   34
a love story in reverse   36
this heart disease called love   39
post-war glamour girl   40
full-time loser   43
the new assassin   44
the it man   47
evidently chicken town   49
the day the world stood still   52
i travel in biscuits   54
salome maloney   56
midnight shift   59
kung fu international   62
36 hours   64
the pest   66
drive she said   68
valley of the lost women   69
gaberdine angus   72
i don't wanna be nice   75
health fanatic   76

track suit   79
sleepwalk   80
beezley street   83
suspended sentence   86
limbo   89
a distant relation   91
the house on nowhere street   92
spilt beans   95
majorca   98
conditional discharge   100
nothing   102
23rd   104
the bronze adonis   105
you never see a nipple in the *daily express*   108
the isle of man   111
night people   112

ten years in an open necked shirt

Lenny Siberia was the bastard offspring of Captain Africa (the lard mogul) and Tracy. The captain disappeared without Tracy who perished alone with her diamond collection, the victim of a mau-mau hit squad, leaving Lenny alone with the one thing money can't buy: poverty.

He was discovered at one year old by a wayward nun; he had been living in the dumb waiter of the zambezi juice bar. Sister James (for it was she) lost no time in mailing the child, by first-class parcel post, to a friend in Brussels. Fortunately he was erroneously delivered to the Eros Luxury Club, a converted charabang in the bowels of Manchester's la quartière latin.

The proprietor, a swarthy ill-mannered character of Armenian origin, received the package with a bestial grunt. Taking a curved knife from a canteen of curved knives, he slashed it open. Lenny gazed into the face of this his first stranger and what he saw was pure malevolence.

He ran down flattened streets patrolled by aimless amputees through a world of refugees, out of the cold war into the deep freeze, he ran out of money, he ran into trouble.

He was adopted by Sheba and Rex, a pair of alsatian dogs who regarded the boy with an uneasy ambivalence. They lived in an Art Deco cocktail cabinet by the bicycle sheds of Salford Metropolitan Police compound. They were devout Catholics.

It was arranged for Lenny to attend the School of Our Lady of the Seven Robes of Gold by the Garden of Sorrows in the Vale of Tears which was run with teutonic efficiency by the little daughters of the sick under the iron rule of Mother Cyrene.

Mother Cyrene was everything rancid to Lenny: her mouth a malignant slit in the murderous mask she called a face; her cheesy breath steaming up his spectacles; her eyes like mobile ball bearings – their colour left a mechanical taste in the mouth.

Daily religious instruction furnished his vacant mind with tales of treachery, morbid betrayals, oceans pink with the blood of multitudes, saints looking to the sky their living bodies smashed by hammers before the alien idols of the heathen. Incense filled his nostrils with the fatal breath of ghosts, hermaphrodite choirs droned in his ears.

Each student could elect to spend their free time in one of three ways: sporting activities, visiting the sick or in the service of the Knights of the Sacred Orchid. The latter seemed the least demanding, the most hygenic and it also appealed to the lad's naïve sense of chivalry.

The Knights of the Sacred Orchid held their thrice-weekly routines in the spacious open-plan lounge of the sinister Raoul, who affected the manner of the proto-fascist with psychotic attention to detail. His navy blue hair sleeked with ancient grease, his meagre Don Ameche moustache waxed stiff like the legs of a dead fly. He went nowhere without the chums.

The chums were namely Horace and Boris, the brothers Morris, a titanic duet each in possession of a powder-blue safari suit and arms of anthropoidal length. Their physical immensity fully emphasized the stiff angular grace of the nifty Raoul who now led the way into the lounge.

The lounge was furnished by three rows of seven leatherette easy chairs faced by one formica table. The curtains were the colour of mustard embellished with the bleeding heart motif. The walls were hung with colourless daubs. The carpet was monotonous, its pattern gave the impression of a small animal crapping at regular intervals. The whole scene was lit by a soundless colour TV and a row of six orange table lamps in which shifting globules of molten wax moved like specimens of rare snot.

Enter Mother Cyrene, flanked by the chums and a hyper-reverent Raoul who wore the look of a man obsessed. She stood on the table and began.

'Even as I speak a filthy tide of bolshevism issues from the dives of tin pan alley in short the world is a subterranean playground for lounge lizards from every sphere of idleness and crime who their pockets a-jingle with Moscow money go unchecked about their evil business take china cathedrals ransacked churches turned into judo schools I have seen the finest laundries in the world converted into bordellos for the gratification of the lumpenproletariat what with the drink trade on its last legs and the land running fallow for want of artificial manures I leave you with this thought . . .'

Mantovani strings cascaded from the Queen Anne Dinatron stereo system. Everyone crossed themselves and left. The chums in their lilac Isetta bubble cars headed for the golden finger bowl where they were employed as part-time knuckle merchants.

Upon arrival at the compound Lenny, to his horror, found the cocktail cabinet in flames and his devoted guardians, Sheba and Rex, their heads split by faceless vigilantes, slaughtered in the rabies scare of '62. 'Christ! Where do I live?' thought Lenny in genuine desperation and the heavy traffic seemed to whisper 'Raoul, Raoul.'

So for two weeks Lenny resided in Raoul's broom cupboard which he shared with an upright vacuum cleaner and Doris the chums' slender loris, a cute little number redolent of the lazoon of Fireball XL5 fame.

Raoul imbued Lenny with the tactile beauty of the luger and the surly prose of Mickey Spillane. Finally, however, it was the prospect of nude fencing lessons that drove Lenny out. Leaving a bag of onions for Doris he left silently via the laundry chute. That winter he got a job at Barmy Sid's Elephants Graveyard of up-to-the-minute accoutrements, during which time he moved into a bathroom with an all-girl cycle gang. On the back of a Woodbine packet in lipstick he wrote this his first poem:

The mopeds head for the seaside
Yvonne
Looked at the trees
And her stomach turned

'That's arguably the greatest poem in the world today,' enthused a sudden voice. Lenny turned round to see a tall, loose-limbed young man dressed in the beatnik anti-mode of the committed; his lank hair was hacked into a careless coup-sauvage style favoured by the existentialists who were A-1 credibilitywise in the flourishing capitals of the EEC. Lenny noticed that although his lips moved his voice seemed to come from the side of his neck.

His name was Reg Trademark, heir to a crumbling biscuit empire who, by virtue of his artistic endeavours, had secured a position of trust at the Marxist-Leninist ping-pong club. He persuaded Lenny to declaim his work the following Thursday at the club's variety night.

Among those appearing were Harry, Barry, Garry and Larry, the Brothers McGarry, reading a three-hour concrete poem entitled 'The Yes No Interlude'; a neo-functionalist mime troupe presenting a two-act play based on 'Stop the World I Wanna Get On': a novel by Larry Dines concerning the Judaeo-Christian ethic of self as not self. Finally, however, it had to be agreed by all that the night belonged to Lenny; agreed by all but Larry Dines who had been poisoned.

In a vain attempt at bourgeois credibility Lenny changed his name to John Cooper Clarke and under this title embarked on a polysyllabic excursion through Thrillsville, UK. Yes, it was be there or be square as, clad in the slum chic of the hipster, he issued the slang anthems of the zip age in the desperate esperanto of the bop. John Cooper Clarke: the name behind the hairstyle, the words walk in the grooves hacking through the hi-fi paradise of true luxury.

euro communist/gucci socialist

for a modern home and cheap electricity
streamlined functional neat simplicity
put yourself on the slum clearance list
dial a dialectical materialist
find out what your net potential is
get married to an existentialist
don't doubt your own identity
dress down to a cool anonymity
the pierre cardin line to infinity
clothes to climb in the meritocracy
the new age of benevolent bureaucracy

i like to visit all the big cities
museums and municipal facilities
i strive for critical ability
i thrive on political activity
i'm alive in a new society
i arrive quickly quietly
the car that i drive is the family variety
roman catholic marxist leninist
happily married to an eloquent feminist
a lapsed atheist all my memories
measure the multitude's deafening density
psycho citizens are my enemies
crypto nazis and their remedies
keep the city silent as the cemetery's
architectural gothic immensity
a new name on the less-than-kosher list
the euro-communist/a gucci socialist

the ghost of al capone

in a marble room i was alone
somewhere in the heart of rome
through gardens long since overgrown
down old arcades of broken stone
i met the ghost of al capone
upon request for some ID
he said the guardian angels are working for me

i call for a cop he said stop or i shoot
one or two holes in your three-piece suit
i say steady on old fruit
he told me not to be so cute
consider the river and the concrete boots
the devil and the deep blue sea
what you saw you didn't see
the guardian angels are working for me

the arms the raving arms
and the hustle and the bustle
muscle in i get sandwiched
between the palms
the waving palms and the banknotes rustle
like an international language

even the recession doesn't put him out of pocket
back in the depression he made a profit
a one-man crime wave who can stop it
the agéd william in his pocket
blackmail blue films narcotics
served with the style of a real neurotic
and the easy smile of a true psychotic
a sort of refugee
from the heart of the apostolic see
from one flat fee to another flat fee
the hours are short and the money's free
and the guardian angels are working for me

i under pressure suggested it
why not confess and quit
you're 39 sir and less than fit
he took my false address and split
by the dirt road through the fever trees
in a lamborghini if you please
to get from a to b
i beat my heart and bend my knee
the guardian angels are working for me

paralysed in precious stone
canonised i stand alone
in the clouds of paradise my home
a million orchids deck the throne
of the man who numbered al capone
the man who numbered all his bones
a personal friend of the sacred three
the guardian angels are working for me

i mustn't go down to the sea again

sunken yachtsmen
sinking yards
drunken scotsmen
drinking hard
every lunatic and his friend
i mustn't go down to the sea again

the ocean drags
its drowning men
emotions flag
me down again
tell tracy babs and gwen
i mustn't go down to the sea again

the rain whips
the promenade
it drips on chips
they turn to lard
i'd send a card if i had a pen
i mustn't go down to the sea again

a string of pearls
from the bingo bar
for a girl
who looks like ringo starr
she's mad about married men
i mustn't go down to the sea again

the clumsy kiss
that ends in tears
how i wish
i wasn't here
tell tony mike and len
i mustn't go down to the sea again

the face behind the scream

this case appears to be urgent
kindly pull the screen
cosmetic surgeon
the son of mister sheen
is jerry building versions
of the face behind the scream

the girl who would be beauty queen
tells the doctor of her dream
in which she reads a magazine
wearing only cold cream
they call her the face behind the scream

the image he maintains
and the silence he observes
say it's worth a little pain
for the figure we both deserve
a cowboy by profession since the age of 17
who's singular obsession is the face behind the scream

the girl who would be beauty queen
tells the doctor of her dream
the soirée in the mezzanine
the castanets and tambourines
a careless word an ugly scene

the doctor knows he's made for good impressions on demand
the new nose in the neighbourhood was fashioned by these hands
he can do it blindfold his instruments are clean
a snapshot in his mind holds the face behind the scream

the girl who would be beauty queen
diamond rivets in her jeans
wild and with it even off screen

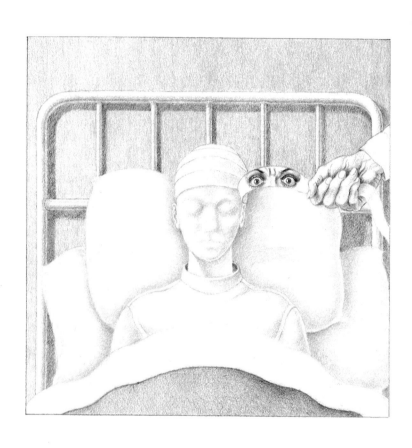

he removes the bandage and the odd remaining scab
a flair for fancy language
the gift of the gab
hands you a sandwich applies the vaseline
to show to best advantage the face behind the scream

the girl who would be beauty queen
tells the doctor of her dream
in which she turns her money green
finds herself in a funny scene
cracks up like a shatterproof windscreen

danke schoen ich liebe dich i promise not to hurt
a telephone receiver clicks RED ALERT
whatever you do don't touch that switch the doctor goes to work
with his bag of tricks in his limousine
mugshots from magazines
face creams and photofits
to fix the face that doesn't fit
the face behind the scream

the girl who would be beauty queen
surrounded by the regular team
of pluto brats and coma teens
in bowler hats and brilliantine
or bold cravats of bottle green
such a precious little dream
to be taken to extremes
how many times can you be 16
they call her the face behind the scream

90 degrees in my shades

i'll be there if you want me
exactly where you said i'd be
in the easy chair
in front of the tv
i don't care what i see
the au pair on the bed settee
with her teddy bear
and a cup of tea
i swear she's out of her tree
the way she stares right out at me
i can't leave i lost my key
i can't breathe somebody help me

visiting the bathroom
that's my format
living in a vacuum
keeps me warm at
90 degrees in my shades
90 degrees in my shades

surprise surprise that monotone phrase
idealise this monochrome haze
i realise these idle days
that come disguised as powder blue rays
hypnotised i only gaze
i cannot rise i can't be phased
square eyes are the latest craze
double size double glazed
i'm stuck in a groove i'll never be free
i can't move somebody help me

boy in the backroom that's my handle
living in a vacuum that's my angle
90 degrees in my shades
90 degrees in my shades

invisible voice now don't forget
you have no choice turn off your set
please mr voice not yet
white noise of a dying pet
any boy's heart would regret
not one spark that i can see
i'm in the dark somebody help me

visiting the bathroom
that's my format
living in a vacuum
keeps me warm at
90 degrees in my shades
90 degrees in my shades

psycle sluts: part one

this disc concerns those pouting prima donnas found within the
rapacious ranks of the sexational psycle sluts – those nubile
nihilists of the north circular the lean leonine leatherette
lovelies of the leeds intersection luftwaffe angels locked in
a pagan paradise – no cash a passion for trash – the tough
madonna whose cro-magnon face and crab nebular curves haunt
the highways of the UK whose harsh credo captures the collective
libido like crazy their lips pushed in the neon arc of a bumper
car – delightfully disciplined dum dum blonde deluxe deliciously
deliciously deranged twin-wheeled existentialists steeped in the
sterile excrement of a doomed democracy whose post nietzschean
sensibilities reject the bovine gregariousness of a senile
oligarchy – condemned to drift like forgotten sputniks in a
fool's orbit bound for the final roadblock fuelled on the
corroding liquids of lurid hopelessness they live for now and
again let the paper tigers flutter in their wake let the last
bastions of the bourgeois quake let the yellow running dog lackies
of imperialism stutter and shake the prayers of the squares
squeal for the merciful oblivion of death and the stormtrooperettes
of les punques nouveaux fifth column close in – on a diet of
dead babies and do-nuts blonde barbarians do not bend their bloody
road – it's woman minus woman revenge by dark degrees – spraycan
manifestoes of one word abound in the pleasure dromes and ersatz
bodega bars of the free world the mechanics of love grind like
organs of iron to a standstill

psycle sluts: part two

the dirty thirty
the naughty forty
the shifty fifty
the filthy five
zips clips whips and chains
wait for you to arrive
bike boys by the bus load
stupid how they strut
smoking woodbines till they're banjoed
smirking at the swedish smut
life on the straight and narrow path
drives you off your nut
by day you are a psychopath
by night you're a psycle slut

on a BSA with two bald tyres
you drove a million miles
you cut your hair with rusty pliers
and suffer with the pillion piles
built in obsolescence
and travel in your guts
you won't reach adolescence
slow down psycle sluts

motorcycle mike
wants to buy a tank
only twenty-nine years old
and he's learning how to wank
yesterday he was in the groove
today he's in a rut
my how the moments move
brute fun psycle sluts

he cacks on your originals
peepee on his boots
he makes love like a footballer
he dribbles before he shoots
the goings on at the gang-bang ball
made the citizens tut tut tut
but what do you care: piss all
you tell 'em psycle sluts

your boyfriend burned his jacket
his ticket expired
his tyres are knackered
and his knackers are tired
tell your tale to the gutter press
get paid to peddle smut
now you've ridden the road of excess
leading to the psycle sluts

or you can dine and whine on stuff
that's bound to give you boils
hot dogs direct from crufts
done in diesel oil
or the burger joint around the bend
where the meals are fast and skimpy
for you that's how the world could end
not with a bang but a wimpy

the day my pad went MAD

somebody came this way and fled
from the heavy wretched scene
all the rooms were grey and red
with an epileptic gleam
i don't know where i'm going
but when i get there i'll be glad
i'm gonna sit right down and write this poem
called the day my pad went MAD

i was ankle deep in human waste
the toilet had been clogged
marrowbone jelly all over the place
i don't even have a dog
the man upstairs he grips my arm
saying don't i know your dad
all i could hear was the fire alarm
the day my pad went MAD

the kitchen had been ransacked
ski trails in the hall
a chicken had been dansacked
and thrown against the wall
in walks this dumb waiter
with a fountain pen and pad
saying how do you want this alligator
the day my pad went MAD

the hamster had been slaughtered
the parrot bound and gagged
the guard dog had been sorted out
and absolutely shagged
the goldfish drowned the cat was found
kicked around and stabbed
the radio did not make a sound
the day my pad went MAD

the pop-up toaster refused to pop
the chandelier was smashed
the starter motor would not stop
the tyres had been slashed
there was no way out of there
i was stuck with what i had
out of order beyond repair
the day my pad went M^{A}D

yesterday i had the place rewired
and i slung out all my junk
a tumble dryer and a two-bar fire
and a telephone now defunct
i peep through the venetian blinds
and the rain fell down so sad
on the broken home i left behind
the day my pad went M^{A}D

i married a monster from outer space

the milky way she walks around
both feet firmly off the ground
two worlds collide two worlds collide
here comes the future bride
give me a lift to the lunar base
i want to marry a monster from outer space

i fell in love with an alien being
whose skin was jelly whose teeth were green
big bug eyes death ray glare
feet like water wings purple hair
i was over the moon
i asked her back to my place
and then i married the monster from outer space

the days were numbered the nights were spent
in a rent-free furnished oxygen tent
a cyborg chef serves up cuisine
the colour of which i've never seen
i needed nutrition to keep up the pace
when i married the monster from outer space

we walked out tentacle in hand
you could sense that the earthlings would not understand
they would whisper when we got on the bus
it's extra-terrestial not like us
it's bad enough with another race
but fuck me a monster from outer space

in a cybernetic fit of rage
she pissed off to another age
she lives in 1999
with her new boyfriend a blob of slime
each time i see a translucent face
i remember the monster from outer space

belladonna

no falling chimes
no call to arms
no siren whines
false alarms
down the telephone lines
at the side of the farms
arm in arm down hemlock row
where the flowers of evil never grow
under one heartbeat heavy but slow
walking together in the purple snow

charming breezes bring the rain
it's gonna run like rats
down the gutters and the drains
it's gonna run like a river
down the window panes
down a web of cracks like twisted veins
a stranger calls my name

between the rollerama and the junk yard
where the panorama looks like mars
and the belladonna looks like stars
behind the panamanian bars
in the dying gardens down below
walking together in the purple snow

withering birds they only wail
drag the waterways to no avail
clutch the steel rails as we go
walking together in the purple snow

no falling chimes
no call to arms
no siren whines
false alarms
down the telephone lines
at the side of the farms
arm in arm down hemlock row
where the flowers of evil never grow
in the dying gardens down below
walking together in the purple snow

i wanna be yours

let me be your vacuum cleaner
breathing in your dust
let me be your ford cortina
i will never rust
if you like your coffee hot
let me be your coffee pot
you call the shots
i wanna be yours

let me be your raincoat
for those frequent rainy days
let me be your dreamboat
when you wanna sail away
let me be your teddy bear
take me with you anywhere
i don't care
i wanna be yours

let me be your electric meter
i will not run out
let me be the electric heater
you get cold without
let me be your setting lotion
hold your hair
with deep devotion
deep as the deep
atlantic ocean
that's how deep is my emotion
deep deep deep deep de deep deep
i don't wanna be hers
i wanna be yours

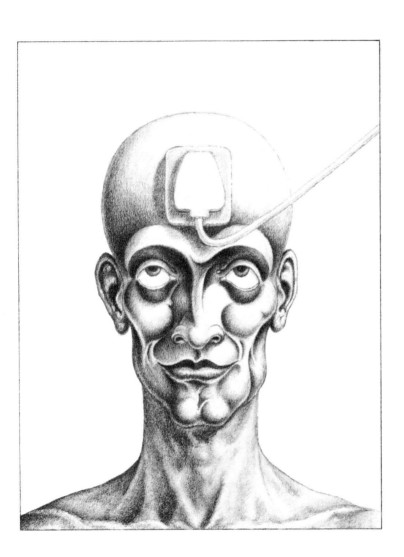

readers' wives

make a date with the brassy brides of britain
the altogether ruder readers' wives
who put down their needles and their knitting
at the doorway to our dismal daily lives

a fablon top scenario of passion
things stick out of holes in leatherette
they seem to be saying in their fashion
i'm freezing charlie have you finished yet

cold flesh the colour of potatoes
in an instamatic sitting room of sin
all the required apparatus
too bad they couldn't get her head in

in latex pyjamas with bananas going ape
identities are cunningly disguised
by a six-inch strip of insulating tape
strategically stuck across their eyes

wives from inverness to inner london
prettiness and pimples co-exist
pictorially wife-swapping with someone
who's happily married to his wrist

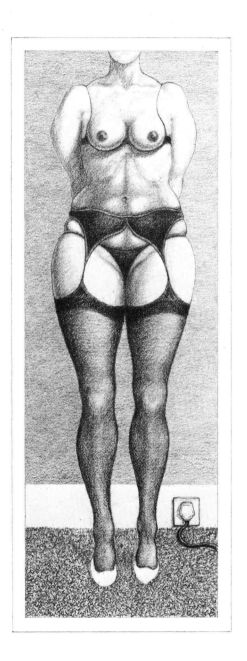

i was a teenage werewolf – or was i

i scream all the way to the chair
and in the face of tanks
i take the stairway to the stairs
and i scream thanks
fake snakes and mock crocs
and killers cut my throat
that's me in the callbox
stepping out of my coat
i've found a reason for living
every day i die
i was a teenage werewolf
or was i

fall off trains
torture dames
i like to keep in the swim
i get slain
on memorex lane
where the people say oh it's him
easy money play hard to get
these love toys to amuse
the non-doctor's penthouse pets
who drink champagne from shoes
walk in rooms and out of rooms
that's my cup of tea
i seen the world i didn't like it
what's in it for me
invisible girls go haywire
i'll be their go-go guy
i was a teenage werewolf
or was i

murder victims talk to me
detectives come and go
their dangling receivers
tell me all i want to know
we only live once or do we
take advice from mickey spillane
me hood nazi blood brother
never give the right name
those dead delicious nudes
they hang around the neck
of a moving raincoat
by the sliding door of a discothèque
where boys are boys and girls are toys
not programmed to reply
i was a teenage werewolf
or was i

a love story in reverse

like a nite klub in the morning
you're the bitter end
like a recently disinfected shithouse
you're clean round the bend
you give me the horrors
too bad to be true
all of my tomorrows
are lousy cos of you
you put the cunt in scunthorpe
you put the pain in spain
happy days are done for
and you're the one i blame
you're certainly no raver
commonly known as a drag
do us all a favour
wear this polythene bag
you're like a dose of scabies
i've got you under my skin
you make life a fairy tale
grimm
a sumo wrestler's armpits
have nothing on your shoes
show me any two half-wits
and they're twice as smart as you
i think about thrombosis
every time we touch
i say you have acute halitosis
you say 'thank you very much'
you're very pleasant
but i know it's just a fad
your very presence
makes me really mad
i hear your knock upon my door
i gotta get out of town
i hit the lights i hit the floor
i turn the TV down

people mention murder
the moment you arrive
i'd consider killing you
if i thought you were alive
you've got this slippery quality
it makes me think of phlegm
and a dual personality
i hate both of them
your bad breath vamps disease
destruction and decay
please please please please
take yourself away
like a death at a birthday party
you have to spoil the fun
like a sucked and spat-out smartie
you're no use to anyone
like a black widow spider
in the shadows of disgrace
speaking as an outsider
what do you think of the human race
you went to a progressive psychiatrist
he recommended suicide
before scratching your bad name off his list
and pointing the way outside
laughter from the playground
breaks your bleeding heart
you're heading for a breakdown
better pull yourself apart
your dirty name is passed about
when something goes amiss
your attitudes are platitudes
they make me want to piss
what kind of creature bore you
was it some kind of bat
they can't find a good word for you
but i can
twat

this heart disease called love

one kiss became a weapon
i don't wanna bleed in vain
clouds collide in the heavens
i surrender to the rain
the death bells that also rang
like madness from above
i'm going out with a bang
and a heart disease called love

ninety-nine below zero
would feel like fever now
you know me: no hero
don't even ask me how
i'm down in the deep deep freeze
what was i thinking of
in the painful breeze
by the frozen trees
with a heart disease called love

after dinner mints
a new lover
and the coffee so bitter and black
your fingerprints
they cover
this knife sticking outa my back
you overlooked the fine detail
you should've worn your gloves
i've got a girl in jail
and a house for sale
and a heart disease called love

post-war glamour girl

expresso bongo snaps of rome
in the latin quarter of an ideal home
fucks all day and sleeps alone
just a tiger rug and a telephone
says a post-war glamour girl's never alone

in the seventh heaven on the thirteenth floor
sweethearts' counterparts kiss
limbo dancers under the door
where the human dynamoes piss
adults only over her pubes
debutantes they give her dubes
beatniks visit with saxophones
and the way she eats that toblerone
says a post-war glamour girl is never alone

mau mau lovers come and go
dreamboats leave her behind
in a baby-doll to go man go
on the slopes of the adult mind
a murder mystery walk-on part
a dead body or a gangland tart
near the knuckle close to home
criminal connections you can't condone
a non-doctor's anonymous drone
says a post-war glamour girl's never alone

that section of the populace
they call the clientele
the moguls of metropolis
defenestrate themselves
in the clothes of a rabbit
you develop a twitch
one of the little sisters of the rich
amorous cameras clamour and click
her rosary beads are really bones
rebel rebel they bug your phone
the post war glamour girl's never alone

40

yes there's always a method actor hanging about
there goes mr tic-tac out the back
with some bric-a-brac from the knick-knack rack
the dumb waiter reminds you of home
and the nice boy from sierra leone
the action painter's got up and gone
nevertheless it's never been known
for a post-war glamour girl ever to be
what you could call
irrevocably
alone

full-time loser

stop that horse
he wears my shirt
regret remorse
o how they hurt
i knock on doors
they turn to dirt
always the beggar
never the chooser
half-clever
full-time loser

from the slumberland
that time forgot
to the wonderland
of a spineless clot
who understands
who calls the shots
you might know
it's another user
part-time poet
full-time loser

the new assassin

skip the roadblock here she comes
get a load of the pretty blue gun
any slick trick under the sun
she'll do it if it isn't done
she made arrangements she couldn't come
she dresses like a secretary lives like a nun
your crime is her radiant passion
it's time for the new assassin

cool killer top of the class
the other side of the shatterproof glass
works fast as the cameras flash
with the cyanide cigarettes and cs gas
it's her job doesn't bat an eyelash
she's working for the perishing mass
the breadline's back in fashion
it's time for the new assassin

a melody played on a hand grenade
from the rifle range in the green arcade
as the rain fell down on the big parade
messed up the motorcade
mucked up the masquerade
secret weapons become displayed
in the hands of half a dozen aides
just four men and a couple of gay blades
shantung suits and shatterproof shades
shoot up anybody who happens to be passing
everybody but the new assassin

one link in a human chain
in the city where it always rains
no profit or personal gain
are the silent rules in a lonesome game
one face in a purple frame
a black border round the name
chalk marks around a blood stain
thin blue line red light flashing
it's time for the new assassin
what time did you see it happen
it's time for the new assassin

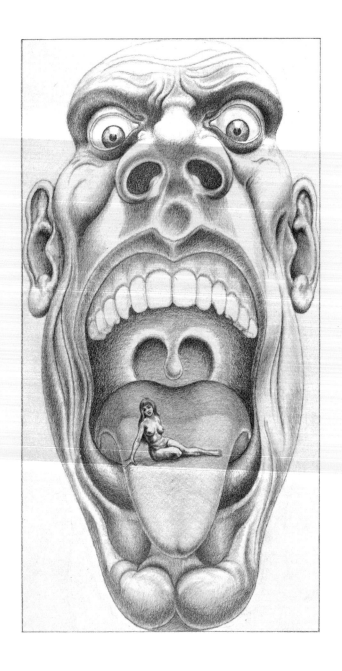

the it man

look who it isn't it's
the it man maybe
the physical description fits
it man baby
you like the julius caesar haircut
middle market leisurewear but
don't let him be your teddy bear
it man baby

you want women wall to wall
it man got
meet the man who started it all
it man got
what's it to be then john
a brunetto or a bleeding blonde
or the telltale tongue of a 2-tone taste bomb
he's the kiddy coming on
like the it man baby

take the sugar round the slums
it's a mug's game
take some bugger for a lump sum
and bugger off to spain

it's an endless stream of fizzy drinks
for it man
whose dentures gleam like digital cufflinks
it man baby
who drove the van
some all purpose also ran
when the shit hits the fan
whose gonna carry the can
for it man

he's after all your stuff
his motto is receive
too much is not enough now
let's not be naive

drip dry zip fly
it man kiss the girls and make them die
it man baby
underneath that yellow shirt
beats a heart of solid dirt
the most disgusting man on earth
it man baby

no back chat was ever written
for it man's tart
the cute cat was a stiff kitten
it man took her apart
he stuck her with a poison pen
next thing news at ten
ladies and gentlemen
it man

well well bloody hell
it man
checking you out and ringing your bell
you'd better quit man
he's walking around taking names
looking for money in the burnt remains
all good stories finish in flames
for it man

evidently chicken town

the fucking cops are fucking keen
to fucking keep it fucking clean
the fucking chief's a fucking swine
who fucking draws the fucking line
at fucking fun and fucking games
the fucking kids he fucking blames
are nowhere to be fucking found
anywhere in chicken town

the fucking scene is fucking sad
the fucking news is fucking bad
the fucking weed is fucking turf
the fucking speed is fucking surf
the fucking folks are fucking daft
don't make me fucking laff
it fucking hurts to look around
everywhere in chicken town

the fucking train is fucking late
you fucking wait you fucking wait
you're fucking lost and fucking found
stuck in fucking chicken town

the fucking view is fucking vile
for fucking miles and fucking miles
the fucking babies fucking cry
the fucking flowers fucking die
the fucking food is fucking muck
the fucking drains are fucking fucked
the colour scheme is fucking brown
everywhere in chicken town

the fucking pubs are fucking dull
the fucking clubs are fucking full
of fucking girls and fucking guys
with fucking murder in their eyes
a fucking bloke is fucking stabbed
waiting for a fucking cab
you fucking stay at fucking home
the fucking neighbours fucking moan
keep the fucking racket down
this is fucking chicken town

the fucking train is fucking late
you fucking wait you fucking wait
you're fucking lost and fucking found
stuck in fucking chicken town

the fucking pies are fucking old
the fucking chips are fucking cold
the fucking beer is fucking flat
the fucking flats have fucking rats
the fucking clocks are fucking wrong
the fucking days are fucking long
it fucking gets you fucking down
evidently chicken town

the day the world stood still

deafening whispers loud and clear
the sound of nothing reached my ears
i get the message and i know the drill
this is the day the world stood still

the day the world stood still
the day the world stood still
no traffic noise or sparrows trill
from the dead flowers on the window sill
this is the day the world stood still

into the mirror stand and stare
like i figure nobody there
time to spare time to kill
this is the day the world stood still

the day the world stood still
the day the world stood still
from the underground to the overspill
no trouble not even at the mill
this is the day the world stood still

specs of dirt and static flies
in spacelike spots before my eyes
a cup of coffee and a couple of pills
this is the day the world stood still

the day the world stood still
the day the world stood still
the big freeze-up gimme a chill
no sense in feeling ill
this is the day the world stood still

i got a whole town to myself
i clear the drugstore shelf by shelf
i couldn't pay i had my fingers in the till
this is the day the world stood still

the day the world stood still
the day the world stood still
drink and drugs and a thousand thrills
from now on it's straight downhill
this is the day the world stood still

i'm falling from the top of my voice
i wreck the vehicles of my choice
a rolls-royce a coupe de ville
this is the day the world stood still

the day the world stood still
the day the world stood still
the last train to clarksville
ran off the rails nobody killed
this is the day the world stood still

i'm driving in a company car
i'm jiving in the tango bar
i'm dining at the luxury grill
this is the day the world stood still

the day the world stood still
the day the world stood still
no trouble not even at the mill
at the end of the day i pay no bill
this is the day the world stood still

i travel in biscuits

the sound of the daylight
the smell of the urine
the rain on the drainpipes
the filthy two-two time
i should know better
how an animal feels
a real go-getter
a wolf on all wheels
white collar whizz kids
button three mohair
i travel in biscuits
getting me nowhere

munchety munch
this is the punchline
crunchety crunch
they last you a lunchtime
who can resist it
who can be so square
i travel in biscuits
getting me nowhere

can you afford it
this is the crunch
orders are audits
a kiss or a punch
a dangerous neighbourhood
don't push it too far
i feel like i'm made of wood
i stay in the car
i have to risk it
i have to go there
i travel in biscuits
getting me nowhere

they keep their crispness
more than just one day
got some for christmas
ate them last monday
if you resist it
i'm gonna go spare
i travel in biscuits
getting me nowhere

the critical daylight
the smell of the urine
the rain on the drain pipes
the filthy two-two time
life is precarious
a long way from home
in alien areas
always alone
i look like a misfit
no one i know there
i travel in biscuits
getting me nowhere

salome maloney

i was walking down oxford road
dressed in what they call the mode
i could hear them spinning all the smash hits
at the mecca of the modern dance: the ritz

feet foxtrotted shoulders did the shimmy
the bouncer on the door said gimme gimme gimme
i gave him the ticket he gave me the shits
no healthy argument it's the ritz

standing by the cig machine who did i see
in lurex and terylene she hypnotised me
i asked her name and she said it's
salome maloney el supremo of the ritz

lacquered in a beehive her barnet didn't budge
wet-look lips smiled as sweet as fudge
she had a number on her back sequins on her tits
the sartorial requirements for women in the ritz

a man making like fred astaire spats and tails
douglas fairbanks moustache dirty fingernails
whose chosen vernacular was subtle as the blitz
charlie macdracula the phantom of the ritz

standing in the dandruff light trying to get pissed
among the headlice old spice brut and bodymist
how could she be seen dead dancing with that prick
and her being salome el supremo of the ritz

a smart move a dangerous curve
sent him arse over bollocks with a body swerve
he started with a cartwheel finished in the splits
leaving salome with his toupee in her mits

tables flew bottles broke the bouncers shouted lumber
the dummy got too chummy in a bing crosby number

the glass globe dropped chopped the crowd to bits
meanwhile what about salome of the ritz

when the ambulances came she was lying on the deck
she fell off her stiletto heels and broke her fucking neck
the band threw down their instruments the management threw fits
she's dead she don't bring the business to the ritz

the over twenty-one's night said it was a shame
the divorcee club will never be the same
joe loss kills himself and vic sylvester quits
when the death dance drama did away with the ritz

the last waltz wilts the quickstep stops
the ladies' excuse me was permanently blocked
and mecca make a living selling little bits
of salome maloney in the wreckage of the ritz

midnight shift

there's a body in the basement
the tv's full of guns
in the room adjacent
cold water runs
the sound of the cisterns
sizzling bacon or chips
footsteps in the distance
she's working on the midnight shift

the room is getting colder
start jumping jack
you're the bluebird over her shoulder
the monkey on her back
she left your taxi fare
there's a message in her gift
you got more than she could spare
she's working on the midnight shift

feedback screams on a twisted riff
luxembourg by night
the cheapjack dream of the midnight shift
doesn't work out right

he's got to shoot he's got to shoot
put his face about
it's like a long abandoned baseball boot
with the tongue hanging out
the perfume of the essence rare
that lingers in the lift
he's a prince among the peasants where
she's working on the midnight shift

you're gonna find her stuck in the lift
to the wonderland of vice
you're gonna find her on the midnight shift
with feet like blocks of ice

she carried water for the mailman
she had to walk the streets
she married the door-to-door salesman
who worked away all week
she lived with an empty chair
until the final rift
she didn't have a thing to wear
she had to work on the midnight shift
you're gonna find her frozen stiff
you think you been hurt
you're gonna find her on the midnight shift
standing in the dirt

you like to put yourself about
like the main man about town
she needs somebody to help her out
but that's where you keep falling down
was there ever a thing so fair
that smashed itself to bits
sometimes you get nowhere
working on the midnight shift

a million tears gonna tear apart
eyes that never shut
a million spears gonna pierce your heart
it's the death of a thousand cuts
a million souls all running scared
or else they only drift
you won't find her anywhere
she's working on the midnight shift

you're gonna find her on the hit list
of a cheapskate beastly rag
you're gonna find her on the midnight shift
what a fuckin drag

you really can't stop now
the visitors arrive
here come the cops now
crunching up the drive
flat footsteps on the stairs
bad news travels swift
sometimes you get nowhere
working on the midnight shift

kung fu international

outside the take-away saturday night
a bald adolescent asked me out for a fight
he was no bigger than a two-bob fart
he was a deft exponent of the martial arts
he gave me three warnings trod on my toes
stuck his fingers in my eyes and kicked me in the nose
a rabbit punch made my eyes explode
my head went dead and i fell in the road
i pleaded for mercy and wriggled on the ground
he kicked me in the balls and said something profound
gave my face the millimetre tread
stole my chop suey and left me for dead
through rivers of blood on fractured bones
i crawled half a mile to the public telephone
pulled a corpse out the call box held back the bile
and with a broken index finger i proceeded to dial
i couldn't get an ambulance the phone was screwed
the receiver fell in half it had been kung fued
a black belt karate cop opened up the door
demanded information about the stiff on the floor
he wore a bamboo mask he was genned on zen
he finished his devotions and he beat me up again
thanks to that embryonic bruce lee
i'm a shadow of the person that i used to be
i can't go back to salford the cops have got me marked
enter the dragon . . . exit johnny clarke

36 hours

36 hours in the mystery chair
36 hours in the quizzical glare
of the naked lights and the visible hardware
another bloke is leaving in a wheelchair
no joke here comes the punchline
lights out sack time

steel shoes on the stone cold floor
i hear the screws screaming in the corridor
the bad news and the slamming of the door
the what did i does and the what am i here fors
shades of doubt fall deeper than the slag mine
lights out sack time

hard cheese and a chest complaint
one man sneezes another two faint
sufferin' jesus this ain't
my venue
the man through the mesh says time to crash
the creeping flesh of a nervous rash
the last man to make a dash
is on the menu

here's the boss with a mouth full of emeralds
a maltese cross and a pocket full of chemicals
jack frost snappin at the genitals
wash my cosh it's a visit from the general
rule out sub section nine
lights out sack time

the killer gorilla with the perspex hat
says i say so and that's that
take out the dog bring back the cat
scrape out the cafeteria rats
stab the rabbit feed the swine
lights out sack time

time flies slides down the walls
part of me dies under my overalls
i close my eyes and a woman calls
from a nightmare
the chronic breath of the dead collides
with the rattle of the waste disposal slides
no flowers for the man who died
in the bombscare
he's in the frigidaire

freezing in these paper jeans
standing stiff in a dead man's dream
tobacco barons and the closet queen
walk on the walls wank in the beans
shave shit a shower and a shoe shine
that's it sack time
everybody looks like ernest borgnine
that's it

36 hours on the battery farm
a blindfold and a broken arm
i got the cold shoulder sleepin' in the barn
who's barn what barn their barn
the old soldier and his old-world charm
lift that weight drag that woodbine
lights out mate sackarooni time
lights out sack time

the pest

the pest pulled up propped his pushbike on a pillar box paused at a post and pissed 'piss in the proper place' pronounced a perturbed pedestrian petulantly and presently this particular part of the planet was plunged into a panorama of public pressure and pleasure through pain the pandemonium prompted the police who patrolled the precinct in pandacars to pull up and peruse the problem while pickpockets picked pockets in pairs 'arrest the pest who so pointedly pissed in that public place' pleaded the peeved populace practically palpitating the powerful police picked up the pest pronounced him a pinko a pansy a punk rocker and a poof they punched him poked him pummeled his pelvis punctured his pipes played ping-pong with his pubic parts and packed him in a place of penal putrifaction he pondered upon progressive politics put pen to paper and provocatively and persuasively propogated his personal political premise – pity: a police provacateur put poison pellets in the pest's porridge the police provocateur was promoted and the pest was presented with the pulitzer peace prize . . . posthumously.

drive she said

i hit the deck
like a ton of lard
when the back of my neck
hit something hard
a yard of lead
or a judo chop
drive she said
i'll tell you when to stop

a morbid silence
filled the air
threats of violence
always there
straight ahead
now take me round the block
drive she said
i'll tell you when to stop

up my sleeve
she stuck me with a spike
said you can leave
whenever i like
give me bread
take me round the shops
drive she said
i'll tell you when to stop

what she cried
i never heard
as colours slide
and voices blurred
the lights were red
stuck on stop
drive she said
i'll tell you when to stop

there was eloquence
style and poise
and pure malevolence
in her voice
move it man
chop chop
drive she said
i'll tell you when to stop

there was eloquence
style and poise
and pure malevolence
in her voice
move it man
chop chop
drive she said
i'll tell you when to stop

she wore leatherette jeans
airwear shoes
i never yet seen
such a rare hairdo
a natty dread
with a borstal crop
drive she said
i'll tell you when to stop

valley of the lost women

the windows are frigidaire icebergs
frozen in prickly heat
the vanishing cream victims
are drip fed amnesia neat
where the test card melodies warm you
in powder blue pseudo bel air
germs and flies alarm you
they whisper the word expelair
the eyes of the night sub zero
peep through the windows of sleep
everyone's husband is a hero
and ghost insurance men creep
through the valley of the long-lost women
dreaming under the driers
eating sleeping and slimming
according to what is required
they walk through three-colour brochures
depicting palms on aqua marine
in the half-built hotels out of focus
they're mending the vending machines
where sixty italian love songs
are sung to a million guitars
they lick their drinks on sticks
among the men with important cigars
numb to the digital numbers
two three . . . four five six
lost in a faraway rhumba
where the oildrums are beaten with sticks

she left her heart in frisco
she left her room in a mess
she left her hat in the disco
she never left her address
the diving board springs to assistance
throws you off from the shore
telephones ring in the distance
there are lifts getting stuck between floors
a truck turns into a cul-de-sac
springtime turns to ice
rucksacks turn into hunchbacks
musclemen turn into mice
in a painless panorama
with its perpendicular might
the women are going bananas
and disappearing from sight

gaberdine angus

gaberdine angus at the magazine rack
views the situation from the front to the back
nobody's looking for the man with the mac
stick it right back on the stack jack

gaberdine angus had a mean trick
had a mean wang made women sick
here's one now go on act the goat
gaberdine angus open your coat

why waste words why risk resistance
when you can climax from a distance
shock tactics designed to stun
gaberdine angus it isn't done

she don't run she don't scream
your pink extremity has gone unseen
she doesn't give the usual nervous cough
so zip up angus and then zip off

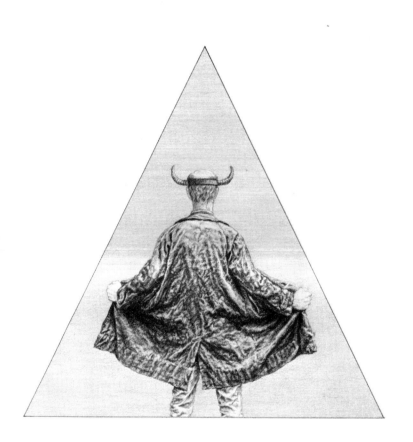

i don't wanna be nice

here he comes now
the fat fingers the expert eyes
the same old how d'you do
disgust is just his dumb disguise
he wants a word with you
his problems are the end
a mouth needs exercise
the last thing i need is another friend
i don't wanna be nice

i don't wanna be nice
i think it's clever to swear
i would seek some sound advice
but i would look elsewhere
what you see is what you get
you only live twice
a friend in need is a friend in debt
i don't wanna be nice

no we never met before
i'm happy to say
far from perfect strangers
i like to keep it that way
i'm not your psychoanalyst
i'd rather talk to mice
you're so easy to resist
i don't wanna be nice

i don't wanna be nice
i think it's clever to swear
i would seek some sound advice
but i would look elsewhere
your face is an obvious case
you shouldn't put it about
this is neither the time nor place
to sort these matters out
what you see is what you get
you only live twice
a friend in need is a friend in debt
i don't wanna be nice

health fanatic

around the block against the clock
tick tock tick tock tick tick tock
running out of breath running out of socks
rubber on the road flippety flop
non-skid agility chop chop
no time to hang about
work out health fanatic work out

the crack of dawn lifting weights
a tell-tale heart reverberates
high in polyunsaturates
low in polysaturates
a duke of edinburgh's award awaits
it's a man's life
he's a health fanatic so was his wife

a one-man war against decay
enjoys himself the hard way
allows himself a mars a day
how old am i what do i weigh
punch me there does it hurt no way
running on the spot don't get too hot
he's a health fanatic that's why not

running through the traffic jam taking in the lead
hyperactivity keeps him out of bed
deep down he'd like to kick it in the head
they'll regret it when they're dead
there's more to life than fun
he's a health fanatic he's got to run

beans greens and tangerines
and low cholesterol margarines
his limbs are loose his teeth are clean
he's a high octane fresh-air fiend
you've got to admit he's keen
what can you do but be impressed
he's a health fanatic give it a rest

shadow boxing punch the wall
one-a-side football
what's the score one all
could have been a copper too small
could have been a jockey too tall
knees up knees up head the ball
nervous energy makes him tick
he's a health fanatic he makes you sick

track suit

two-tone stretch nylon yellow stripes on navy blue
i got a brand new track suit i got the old one too
i got the old one too

i got a new track suit
i wear it every day
keeps me cool and casual
i wore it yesterday
i wore it yesterday

i got a new track suit
i wear it everywhere
track me down to the training ground
maybe i'll be there
maybe i'll be there

wearing the brand new track suit
medicine ball to boot
knee pads an airline bag
and the overall smell of brut
the overall smell of fruit

expert eyes have scrutinized
and scientists agree
one track suit would suffice
but you're better off with three
you're better off with three

two-tone stretch nylon yellow stripes on navy blue
i got a brand new track suit i got the old one too
i got the old 1 . . . 2

sleepwalk

i can wriggle out of arrangements you can't pin me down
i tend to dodge engagements i'll see you around
am i OK not really no i seem to stop and start
anything i can do let me know i think i'll sleepwalk outta my heart

sleepwalk in the daytime access to all floors
sleepwalk in a straight line leading out of the door
shockproof city a world of eyes marvellously dead
these friends of mine need exercise they sleepwalk instead

no guardian angel intercepts the sleepwalking kid
who sleepwalks the fractured steps to the sleepwalking skids
the way the private eye goes about his ancient art
i can do it with my eyes closed sleepwalk outta my heart

stop look listen to the zombie the hootchie kootchie blues
black slacks and a crombie gucci shoes
a psycho stud and his steady girl are heading right this way
when all the footsteps in the world sleepwalk away

the victim of ambition loitering with intent
the human condition of who knows what percent
it's goodbye from me till now i never really cared
sleepwalk anyhow anywhere

sleepwalk talk faster and faster one of these talking birds
sleepwalk away from disasters like they never occurred
too much devotion keeps me apart
sleepwalk in slow motion outta my heart

in the creepy zilch of subways the sub pedestrian plod
sleepwalk on sunday beneath the drones of god
such a hazardous pastime i'm gonna be smart
sleepwalk for the last time outta my heart

sleepwalk on duty see myself in a pool
a sleepwalking cutie a sleepwalking fool
stuck in the afternoon they do go on
when normal service is resumed i'll be sleepwalking gone

beezley street

far flung crazy pavements crack
the sound of empty rooms
a clinical arrangement
a dirty afternoon
where the fecal germs of mr freud
are rendered obsolete
the legal term is null and void
in the case of beezley street

in the cheap seats where murder breeds
somebody is out of breath
sleep is a luxury they don't need
a sneak preview of death
deadly nightshade is your flower
manslaughter your meat
spend a year in a couple of hours
on the edge of beezley street

where the action isn't
that's where it is
state your position
vacancies exist
in an x certificate exercise
ex servicemen explete
keith joseph smiles and a baby dies
in a box on beezley street

from the boarding houses and the bedsits
full of accidents and fleas
somebody gets it
where the missing persons freeze
wearing dead men's overcoats
you can't see their feet
a riff joint shuts and opens up
right down on beezley street

cars collide colours clash
disaster movie stuff
for the man with the fu manchu moustache
revenge is not enough
there's a dead canary on a swivel seat
there's a rainbow in the road
meanwhile on beezley street
silence is the mode

it's hot beneath the collar
it's cold beneath the balls
where the perishing stink of squalor
impregnates the walls
the rats have all got rickets
they spit through broken teeth
a blood stain is your ticket
one way down beezley street

the gangster and his hired hat
drive a borrowed car
he lookes like the duke of edinburgh
but not so lah-di-dah
OAP mother-to-be
watch that three-piece suite
when shitstopper drains
and crocodile skis
are seen on beezley street

in the kingdom of the blind
where the one-eyed man is king
beauty problems are redefined
the doorbells do not ring
light bulbs pop like blisters
the only form of heat
where a fellow sells his sister
down the river on beezley street

the boys are on the wagon
the girls are on the shelf
their common problem
is that they're not someone else
the dirt blows out
the dust blows in
you can't keep it neat
it's a fully furnished dustbin
16 beezley street

vince the ageing savage
betrays no kind of life
but the smell of yesterday's cabbage
and the ghost of last year's wife
through a constant haze
of deodorant sprays
he says retreat
alsatians dog the dirty days
down the middle of beezley street

eyes dead as viscous fish
look around for laughs
if i could have just one wish
i would be a photograph
on this permanent monday morning
get lost or fall asleep
when the yellow cats are yawning
round the back of beezley street

people turn to poison quick
as lager turns to piss
sweethearts are physically sick
every time they kiss
it's a sociologist's paradise
each day repeats
uneasy cheesy greasy queasy beastly beezley street

suspended sentence

read the paper humdrum
what's the caper what goes on
eat die ho hum
page one some bum
is giving a lunatic a loaded gun
he walks others run
thirty dead no fun
do something destructive chum
sit right down write a letter to the sun
bring back hanging for everyone

they took my advice they brought it back
the national costume was all over black
there were corpses in the avenues and cul-de-sacs
piled up neatly in six-man stacks
hanging from the traffic lights and specially made racks
they'd hang you for incontinence and fiddling your tax
failure to hang yourself justified the axe
deedley dee deedley dum
they brought back hanging for everyone

the novelty's gone it's hell
the whole place is a death cell
the bang bang bang of the funeral bells
those who aren't hanging are hanging someone else
the people pay the paper sells
death by the lorry load it smells
swinging britain don't put me on
they brought back hanging for everyone

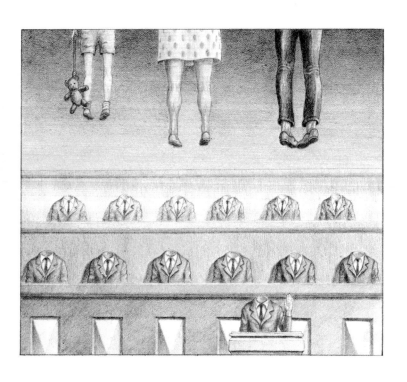

limbo

their lives are a mystery they make it their career
in the single file of history fall and disappear
swearing they'll get even with all those other creeps
philistines and heathens who violently sleep
or steal from cigarette machines just for the change
to get back to where they've been: a doorway in the rain

back in the confession box back in the slums
desire burns like chicken pox underneath the thumbs
a refugee from purgatory in a purple robe of scorn
in the holy ghost observatory wears a crown of thorns
turns out she's a gringo a hard circumstance
limbo baby limbo they wanna see you dance

take the tradesmen's entrance take it out on a tramp
every fucking sentence complaints about the damp
the only girl is a faint cry from a garden of cement
weekends watch the paint dry it's a big event
look through heaven's windows with their opalescent panes
limbo baby limbo down the boulevard of shame

saint margaret dies intact she hardly seems alert
the marble glance denies the fact her face hurts
the extra legal image the cold cream skin
the regal gimmicks did you in
look through heaven's windows you can see the powder blue veil
the cover girl of limbo and sweetheart of the jail

gipsy babies hopscotch outside the silver gates
the witch doctor's wrist watch is stuck at five to eight
a bad break a slight ache is everyone's complaint
flesh flakes like angel cake from mugshots of the saint
who fell from a window and was never seen again
till he turned up in limbo: a doorway in the rain

a hero rides to heaven the public merely rot
for a fraction of forever in a designated spot
eternally paralysed the morbid orbit shifts
halfway to paradise stuck in the lift
some smart cracking bimbo says you can't be employed
sends you off to limbo on the stairway to a void

a distant relation

a family affair
look at this picture
we're in there somewhere
permanent fixtures
people who care
stranger beware
this is a family affair

all of our yesterdays
familiar rings
i have to get away
it's breaking my heart strings
we have a drink
it's a special occasion
it makes me think
about a distant relation

a family affair
always a mixture
of people in chairs
permanent fixtures
bring pressure to bear
and problems to share
this is a family affair

holiday snapshots
of you and myself
acting like crackpots
like everyone else
the bermuda shorts
and the summer creations
bringing thoughts
of that distant relation

a family affair
we break ornaments
and get them repaired
we bring up past events
that hang in the air
stranger beware
this is a family affair

all of our yesterdays
familiar rings
i have to get away
from certain surroundings
weddings and funerals
and special occasions
and all the usual
distant relations

a family affair
look at this picture
we're in there look there
permanent fixtures
people who care
whisper who dares
this is a family affair

the house on nowhere street

only a graze was the final phrase
running out of breath
a travelling javelin stabbed him in the abdomen
he bled to death
the poor fool he found his feet
but left his face behind
in the happy house on nowhere street
with the pale blue bamboo blind

the trembling tongues he once enjoyed
talk behind his back
tell me he was self employed
he gave himself the sack
he's on the scrounge in the cocktail lounge
where once he wined and dined
a thousand eyeballs shake him down
from the pale blue bamboo blind

the music will continue
there is no way out
bone muscle and sinew
begin to move about
whip that sucker with a heavy back beat
you gotta be cool to be the kind
who haunt the house on nowhere street
with the pale blue bamboo blind

he's hanging round the swimming pool
with a mental cigarette
he knows what keeps all women cool
he knows what gets 'em wet
wave on wave of body heat
frozen in his mind
far from the house on nowhere street
with the pale blue bamboo blind

he came in search of paradise
he even learned to drive
became a living sacrifice
to other people's wives
nobody seeks similar
with nothing much in mind
apply the house on nowhere street
with the pale blue bamboo blind

spilt beans

the roads are littered with guilty men
who write your name with a poison pen
one by one those friendly swine
who fell off the bent assembly line
turn up for a cup of tea
turn up the colour TV
then they put it about that you've been mean
it's no good crying over spilt beans

all those fancy dans at the palais de danse
offer you assistance in their firm's vans
nice boys who love their mothers
much more than a million lovers
what he wants is four spare wheels
one fair deal and two square meals
he's exactly as he seems
it's no good crying over spilt beans

he's got sixty low-down dirty ways
to drive you mad in thirty days
you give him a rose he gives you thorns
you give him poetry he gives you porn
you give him presents he sends them back
he got a seven-course dinner said thanks for the snack
give me what's crucial crisp and green
it's no good crying over spilt beans

the three stooges the four just men
the magnificent seven and the hollywood ten
lord rockingham's eleven and the famous five
three men in a boat and their wives
the twelve apostles and the fiddlers three
ten green bottles and the three degrees
and wave on wave of brilliantine
says no good crying over spilt beans

indigestion housemaid's knees
your complexion looks like cheese
you make groovy gravy mother of meat
since you wed all you do is eat
too fat to fuck and that's that
he's got genitals fitted with a thermostat
a hitch in the kitchen what's that scream
it's no good crying over spilt beans

majorca

fasten your seat belts says the voice
inside the plane you can hear no noise
engines made by rolls-royce
take your choice
make mine majorca

check out the parachutes can't be found
alert the passengers they'll be drowned
a friendly mug says settle down
when i come round i'm gagged and bound
for majorca

here comes the neat hostess
and her unapproachable flip finesse
i found the meaning of the word excess
they've got little bags if you want to make a mess
i fancied cuba but it cost a lot less
to majorca
(whose blonde sand fondly kisses the cool fathoms
of the blue mediterranean)

they packed us into the white hotel
you could still smell the polycell
and the white paint in the air-conditioned cells
the waiter smells of fake chanel
gauloises garlic as well
said if i like i could call him miguel
well really

i got drunk with another fella
who'd just brought up a previous paella
wanted a fight but said they were yella
in majorca

the guitars rang the castinets clicked
the dancers stamped the dancers kicked
the double diamond flowed like sick
mother's pride tortilla and chips
pneumatic drills you can't kip
take a dip you're in the shit
if you sing in the street you're knicked
in majorca

the heat made me sick i had to stay in the shade
must have been something in the lemonade
but by the balls of franco i paid
i had to pawn my bucket and spade
next year i take the international brigade
to majorca

conditional discharge

satisfaction comes and goes
biological action cannot be froze
a sexual recharge a plug in a socket
conditional discharge a sticky deposit

love on the sick down in the dumps
visit the clinic where the microscopes jump
with the love-sick side effects tell me what was it
conditional discharge a sticky deposit

the memory lingers of a clean routine
another man's fingers under my jeans
he gave me a card some antibiotics
said conditional discharge a sticky deposit

a random fuck dirty sheets
a crack in a cup a lavatory seat
i'm in the dark about where i got it
conditional discharge a sticky deposit

sexual freedom left me alone
in a garden of eden syndrome
it's on the cards you'll come across it
conditional discharge a sticky deposit

the ups and downs of times like these
fucking around is a social disease
and the public at large don't know they've got it
conditional discharge a sticky deposit

a problem of leisure measured in terms
of pain plus pleasure plus poison sperm
take this diagram keep it in your pocket
conditional discharge sticky deposit

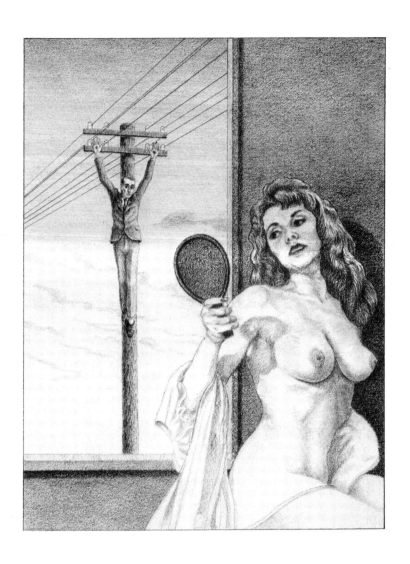

nothing

nothing isn't anything
it's tasteless and it's flat
nothing if it's anything
is even less than that
i've got that certain nothing
no one can do without
the spanish call it nada
i call it nowt
i'd take the train but don't care
to travel by myself
all the way from nowhere
to get to nowhere else
nothing ever goes on
nothing never ends
say nothing to no one
it's nothing to do with them
nothing going on and on
nothing wall to wall
it happens once and then it's gone
leaving bugger all

23rd

you can count on him
he'll always let you down
while you hang about for him
he's in another town
he gets from A to B
he can't see eye to eye
with anyone if you ask me
he doesn't try

check his empty pockets
check them more than once
he hasn't got it
whatever it is that you want
energy is a four-letter word
he doesn't buy
here he comes now 23rd
he doesn't try

compassion it isn't necessary
his sickness is an act
he'll make you an accessory
after this obvious fact
you must excuse him
ask his mother why
you can't use him
he doesn't try

it doesn't pay to help him
he's somewhere else
tell him you can't tell him
he's a fool to himself
what's in it for me
you know the kind
always saying why
two weeks behind
he doesn't try

bikes buses trucks and trains
gangways ladders and ramps
a seemingly endless chain
of pickpockets and tramps
he wears the look of false alarm
like an old school tie
someone ought to twist his arm
he doesn't try

laugh it isn't funny
no respect for pain
if you give him money
he slings it down the drain
you're looking for mr right
his type need not apply
he won't play the white man
he doesn't try

the bronze adonis

she did not like the rib-cage
the coat hanger hips
the razor-sharp shoulder blades
give her jip
she's reading edward de bono under the palms
he sprays odorono under the arms
i was to say the least alarmed
when the bronze adonis got her

i lay beneath the parasol
watched him with the chicks
horsing around with his aerosol
they whispered about his odd trick
send no cash fear no man
you can be a love leviathan
she's a fan of the man with a tan from a can
the bronze adonis got her

they honeymoon on muscle beach
to cries of 'beat it mac'
he plucks some puny pansy's peach
well how do you like that
the bronze adonis got her

mr and mrs universe
the folks who live in the gym
each night she sleeps in a room marked her
he sleeps in a room marked him
muscle bound for stardom the apollo of your eye
can't seem to get a hard on o christ i wonder why
the bronze adonis got her

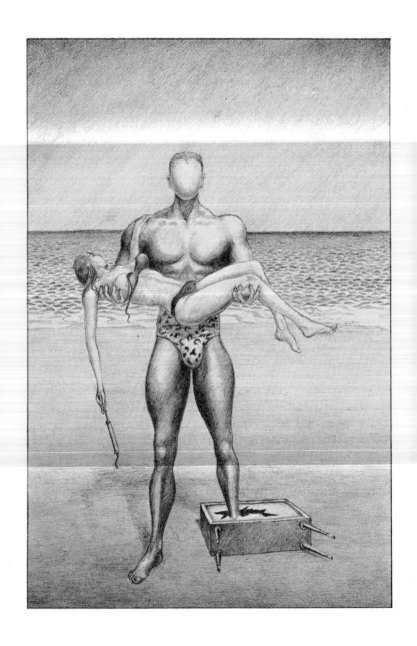

there stands the body gorgeous
men worship girls admire
he bravely bears the scourges
and the squelch of squashed desire
what a physical jerk no time for sex
where's me bleeding bullworker baby oil and leopard kecks
o yeah the bronze adonis got her

a mail-order male
let me show you how
fragile frankie frail
becomes agile al kapow
the he-man hero blond and tall the envy of his pals
he's coming to burst your beach ball and wrestle with your gals
is this the viscose vaseline dream or a triumph of the will
when the bronze adonis gets her downtown palookaville

hubba hubba yum yum wow
what a hunk of beef
who made you the sacred cow
who hangs around his briefs
in the corner sauna with his mates
wanking away unwanted weight
that's his idea of a heavy date
the bronze adonis got her

you never see a nipple in the *daily express*

i've seen the poison letters of the horrible hacks
about the yellow peril and the reds and the blacks
and the tuc and its treacherous acts
kremlin money – all right jack
i've seen how democracy is under duress
but i've never seen a nipple in the *daily express*

i've seen the suede jack boot the verbal cosh
whitehouse whitelaw whitewash
blood uptown where the vandals rule
classroom mafia scandal school
they accuse i confess
i've never seen a nipple in the *daily express*

agony columns scream in pain
love in vain domestic strain
divorce disease it eats away
the family structure day by day
in the grim pursuit of happiness
i've never seen a nipple in the *daily express*

this paper's boring mindless mean
full of pornography the kind that's clean
where william hickey meets michael caine
again and again and again and again
i've seen millionaires on the dhss
but i've never seen a nipple in the *daily express*

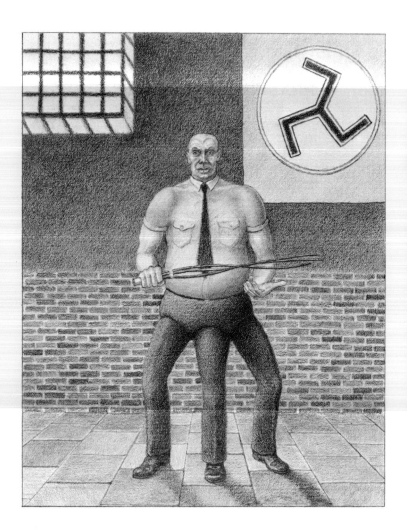